David Roberts

First published: October 2015
Text © David Roberts 2015
This edition © Red Planet Publishing Ltd 2015
ISBN: 9781905959778

Design: Mark Young
Editor: Matt Milton
Publisher: Mark Neeter
Proof reader Matt White
Front cover photo: Simon Emmett

For more information visit: www.redplanetzone.com

David Roberts

THE STARS (IN ORDER OF APPEARANCE)

CHUCK BERRY
MORRISSEY
DAVID CASSIDY
KEITH RICHARDS
JON BON JOVI
JIM MORRISON
DEBBIE HARRY
THE MONKEES
KEITH MOON
GEORGE HARRISON
JOHN LENNON
BRUCE
SPRINGSTEEN
WILL.I.AM
MICK JAGGER
SNOOP DOGG
SONNY & CHER
ROGER DALTREY
BOBBY DARIN
U2
BILL WYMAN
KATE BUSH
ROD STEWART
DIANA ROSS
MARVIN GAYE

ELVIS PRESLEY
RUN-DMC
JAMES BROWN
SYD BARRETT
PINK FLOYD
NICK MASON
CAPTAIN
BEEFHEART AND
HIS MAGIC BAND
BOB DYLAN
PAUL WELLER
BILLY GIBBONS
DAVID RUFFIN
BARRY GIBB
FREDDIE MERCURY
DENNIS WILSON
GRAM PARSONS
JANIS JOPLIN
THE KINKS
PAT BENATAR
BRIAN JONES
LIAM GALLAGHER
HANK WILLIAMS
RY COODER
BRIAN WILSON

ROY ORBISON
GLENN FREY
JACKSON BROWNE
JAY KAY
NEIL YOUNG
ALEX CHILTON
CREEDENCE
CLEARWATER
REVIVAL
BEYONCE AND JAY Z
USHER
RINGO STARR
ALICE COOPER
OZZY AND SHARON
OSBOURNE
BRIAN JOHNSON
TEARS FOR FEARS
ELTON JOHN
SLASH
SHARKS
KYLIE MINOGUE
BOB DYLAN
BRYAN FERRY
T.I.
STEPHEN STILLS &

PETER TORK
THE DAVE CLARK
FIVE
SAMMY HAGAR
MUDDY WATERS
TRIPLE C'S
FLO RIDA
JIMI HENDRIX
THE MOTHERS OF
INVENTION
FRANK ZAPPA
MOTÖRHEAD
ISAAC HAYES
NEIL YOUNG AND
DANIEL LANOIS
JOE STRUMMER
MICK FLEETWOOD
TOM PETTY
LED ZEPPELIN
WILLIE NELSON
STEVEN TYLER
TAYLOR SWIFT
RONNIE LANE

THE CARS

FORD THUNDERBIRD
FIAT 500
CORVETTE STINGRAY
BENTLEY S3
CHEVROLET
CHEVELLE
SHELBY MUSTANG
GT500
CHEVROLET CAMARO
THE MONKEEMOBILE
FERRARI DINO 246
ASTON MARTIN DB5
ROLLS-ROYCE
PHANTOM V
CHEVROLET CORVETTE
TESLA ROADSTER
ASTON MARTIN DB6
PONTIAC PARISIENNE
FORD MUSTANGS
CADILLAC
CONVERTIBLE
THE 'DREAM CAR'
(DIDIA 150)
TRABANT
CITROEN SM

(IN ORDER OF APPEARANCE)

FERRARI 308 GTS
ENZO FERRARI
ROLLS-ROYCE
CORNICHE
ROLLS-ROYCE
PHANTOM
CADILLAC ELDORADO
LINCOLN CONTINENTAL
PONTIAC PARISIENNE
GP BEACH BUGGY
FERRARI 250 GTO
AUTO UNION TYPE C
CADILLAC SERIES 62
CHEVROLET MASTER
BMW MINI COOPER
FORD THUNDERBIRD
MYSTERY BLACK
SALOON
LOTUS EUROPA
STUDEBAKER
CHAMPION
CHEVROLET ONE-FIFTY
CADILLAC ELDORADO
PORSCHE 365
BUICK ELECTRA 225

NASH AMBASSADOR
ROLLS-ROYCE
SILVER CLOUD
BRISTOL
CADILLAC
BUICK CONVERTIBLE
CHEVROLET CORVETTE
STINGRAY
EXCALIBUR ROADSTER
CHEVROLET BEL AIR
CADILLAC SERIES 62
CADILLAC ELDORADO
BIARRITZ
CADILLAC ELDORADO
CONVERTIBLE
RAMBLER CLASSIC
660 STATION WAGON
ROLLS-ROYCE
PHANTOM V
MGB GT
MGB ROADSTER
MG MGA ROADSTER
PONTIAC FIREBIRD
MASERATI
BUICK SKYLARK

CHEVROLET IMPALA
CABRIOLET DELUXE
MERCEDES A45 AMG
MERCEDES-BENZ
600 PULLMAN
MERCEDES-BENZ 600
DODGE MONACO
SEDAN
CADILLAC DE VILLE
FORD THUNDERBIRD
CADILLAC DE VILLE
FERRARI 275 GTB
LAMBORGHINI MIURA
CHEVROLET BEL AIR
CHEVROLET BEL AIR
OLDSMOBILE
FUTURAMIC
ROLLS-ROYCE
BENTLEY VANDEN
PLAS LE MANS
TOURER
CHEVROLET CORVETTE
FORD MUSTANG
FERRARI DINO 246
JAGUAR E-TYPE

FERRARI ENZO
CHEVROLET CORVETTE
STINGRAY
PONTIAC LE MANS
LEXUS CT 200H
CADILLAC ESCALADE
MESSERSCHMITT
KR200
BENTLEY MULSANNE
BENTLEY S
AUSTIN PRINCESS
JAGUAR E-TYPE
FERRARI 599
GTB FIORANO
CADILLAC FLEETWOOD
60 SPECIAL SEDAN
CADILLAC ELDORADO
SEVILLE
BUGATTI VEYRON
ROLLS-ROYCE
SILVER WRAITH
VOLVO P1800
FORD DEUCE COUPE
BARRIS CUSTOM
FERRARI 250

CALIFORNIA SPYDER
CADILLAC CUSTOM
('49–'70)
LOTUS ELAN
DODGE PICK-
UP TRUCK
D-7 TRACTOR
FORD CAPRI
STUTZ BLACKHAWK
LINCOLN CONTINENTAL
CHRYSLER MONARCH
BUSINESS COUPE
DESOTO FIREDOME
SPORTSMAN
NISSAN FIGARO
1939 PACKARD
JAGUAR XJS
JAGUAR XK150
DODGE PICK-UP
1956 MERCEDES
220 CONVERTIBLE
1949 DODGE
WAYFARER
FORD BRONCO
LAND ROVER

CHUCK BERRY
FORD THUNDERBIRD

The Thunderbird is a
Fifties American classic.
All the rock 'n' rollers had
one – Elvis, Gene Vincent,
Bill Haley and, of course,
Chuck Berry. Powered by a
300-horsepower V8 engine,
Chuck's late-Fifties convertible
had a 150-mph speedometer.

Chuck paid homage to
his T-Bird on 'Jaguar &
Thunderbird', singing: *"Keep
cool, little Thunderbird
Ford / Ten miles stretch
on an Indiana Road."*.

MORRISSEY
FIAT 500

You'd think the vegan Smiths singer would be more of a cyclist than a petrolhead. But he did once sing: "*I don't want a lover, I just want to be tied to the back of your car*" (from 'You've Got Everything Now').

His Fiat 500 is the slightly larger "estate" model known as the 'Giardiniera', produced between 1960 and 1975 (and possibly also the name of Mozza's favourite pizza). Its rear doors are nicknamed "suicide doors" – hinged at the back, they open in a way more likely to lead to falling out of the car.

BOYS ON THE HOOD

DAVID CASSIDY
CORVETTE STINGRAY

The 70s teen idol (aka "Keith Partridge" from TV's *The Partridge Family*) lounges barefoot on his curvy Corvette in 1973.

KEITH RICHARDS
BENTLEY S3

The Stones guitarist with his 1966 'Blue Lena' S3 Continental, named after the jazz singer Lena Horne. Keith drove it to Morocco in 1967 with Anita Pallenberg and her boyfriend Brian Jones. By their return, Anita was with Keith.

JON BON JOVI
CHEVROLET CHEVELLE

When Jon wanted a 1970 Chevelle Convertible, he hired the specialists at Obie's Hot Rods to track one down. They found this beauty in southern Georgia.

BEHIND THE WHEEL

JIM MORRISON
SHELBY MUSTANG GT500

A gift from his record company, Morrison's mist-blue 67 Mustang is a great lost rock 'n' roll treasure. Nobody knows where it is; it disappeared shortly before Jim's death in Paris. Some say Jim abandoned it on Sunset Boulevard after he drove it into a lamp-post. Others believe it was auctioned after he left it too long at LAX airport whilst on tour. The Doors singer can be seen driving it in the movie *HWY: An American Pastoral.*

DEBBIE HARRY
CHEVROLET CAMARO

In early 70s New York, the Blondie singer drove a classic Camaro coupe, inherited from her mother. Its front eventually caved in after too many parking prangs; the scrapyard wouldn't take it and it was pushed off a cliff. We presume the car was stationary when this photo was taken, and that Debbie doesn't weirdly steer by balancing her left arm on top of the wheel...

THE MONKEES
THE MONKEEMOBILE

The car that spawned millions of model kits and diecast toy models, the greatly customised Pontiac GTO was the transportation of Sixties 'manufactured' band The Monkees, who ruled the trans-Atlantic TV airways in 1966-1968.

KEITH MOON
FERRARI DINO 246

What must his car insurance premiums have looked like?! Definitely a car for the wildest Keiths of rock: Keith Richards was a fan and so was Keith Moon. But in The Who drummer's defence, the totalling of this little beauty was absolutely, categorically, NOT his fault! Moon, who had only taken delivery of the Dino a few weeks previously, was enjoying a pint or two at his local, The Golden Grove in Chertsey, when a couple of young bikers stopped to admire his new set of wheels. Encouraging them to take it for a spin, the two lads eagerly accepted but quickly found the Dino too hot to handle and sent it crashing into a deep roadworks ditch.

FAB FIVES

GEORGE HARRISON
ASTON MARTIN DB5

An 007-like pose by Aston Martin-loving George outside his Surrey bungalow, Kinfauns.

JOHN LENNON
ROLLS-ROYCE PHANTOM V

The most expensive car in the world when sold at a Sotherby's auction in 1985 for $2.3 million, John Lennon's Rolls-Royce started life as a Valentines Black model until a visit to a fairground in 1967 sparked an idea by Ringo Starr. The drummer suggested his fellow Beatle have his two-year-old car painted in a psychedelic livery inspired by the fairground artwork. A local Chertsey coachworks company were hired to complete the car's transformation using the gypsy caravan in Lennon's garden in Weybridge as a design guide. Lennon's Roller also featured early innovations such as blacked-out windows, an in-car record player and a TV set.

BRUCE SPRINGSTEEN
CHEVROLET CORVETTE

Acquired on the back of a ton of sales for his *Born to Run* album in 1975, Bruce's 1960 Chevrolet Corvette is parked on Colonial Avenue, Haddonfield, New Jersey. This picture was one of a number of shots from The Boss' photo session with photographer Frank Stefanko on an icy cold day in 1978.

WILL.I.AM
TESLA ROADSTER

No offence Chris Evans, but those BBC TV *Top Gear* bosses really should have given the gig to will.i.am. Not only is he a self-confessed petrolhead, he likes ranking cars in his own lists. Zooming up that chart is the Tesla electric car, capable of just shy of 250 miles on one single charge and 0-60 mph in under four seconds. Tesla is "right up there" with the best of them, according to the LA-born music mogul. The full will.i.am high performance car Top 10 looks like this: McLaren, Lamborghini, Bugatti, Ferrari, Lotus, Tesla (to his right), Maserati, Bentley (behind him), Mercedes-Benz and BMW.

PRISTINE TO PRANG

MICK JAGGER
ASTON MARTIN DB6

Mick looks his inscrutable best for a photo session with top photographer Gered Mankowitz in the summer of 1966. A trendy Marylebone cobbled mews was the setting for the shoot, where Mick showed off his new midnight blue Aston Martin DB6. The Grand tourer, with its 3995cc engine, had been launched at the London Motor Show only a year earlier, and the recent success of The Rolling Stones' No 1 album *Aftermath* and chart-topping single 'Paint it Black' had provided Mick with enough cash to splash on a car that matched his fashionable man-about-London image. What a drag, then, that his pride and joy should end up in a costly collision so soon. Rock aristocracy collided with the real thing when Mick (along with passenger girlfriend Chrissie Shrimpton) were involved in a prang with the Countess of Carlisle, travelling in a Ford Anglia.

"I only bought the car three months ago," said a disconsolate Jagger. "The damage is going to cost £200."

I GOT YOU BABE

SNOOP DOGG
PONTIAC PARISIENNE

Snoop's 1967 convertible isn't just yellow on the outside. The dashboard's yellow, the sumptuous seats are yellow and even the steering wheel is yellow. The hood has been signed by LA Lakers basketball players. As *Lowrider* magazine so brilliantly put it, this is probably Snoop's favourite among his "automotive harem".

SONNY & CHER
FORD MUSTANGS

Created to reflect the personalities of husband and wife singing duo Sonny Bono and Cher, this pair of 1966 Mustangs came in two sizes. As a publicity stunt, it must have been an expensive one. Cher's pink 'Stang' included ermine and Scottish leather upholstery and a white fur-lined trunk. Sonny's more soberly designed brown theme featured antique leather, funky suede and bobcat fur seats.

FINS AIN'T WHAT THEY WERE

ROGER DALTREY
CADILLAC CONVERTIBLE

Shame on you Roger. It's like the Archbishop of Canterbury defecting to Satan! The Who frontman turns greaser/rocker and forgoes the pleasure of a Mod Vespa or Lambretta for this 1959 Cadillac Series 62 convertible. A vision in pink and chrome, those fins advertised to the rest of the world that the US automobile industry was not only the biggest but the best in the world back in 1959.

BOBBY DARIN
THE 'DREAM CAR'

The DiDia 150 was a one-off. Simply known as the 'Dream Car', this automotive folly took four men four years to build before singer Bobby Darin bought it in 1961 for $150,000. Named after its designer, Andy Di Dia, the car was propelled by a 365 cubic-inch Cadillac V8 engine and was covered in 30 coats of paint mixed with ground diamonds for sparkle.

U2
TRABANT

With the release of their 1991 album *Achtung Baby,* U2 swerved away from their love-affair with American roots music and went all Eastern European. As a basic symbol of what they were about at the time, the bog-standard East German Trabant was the perfect fit and featured on the LP cover and subsequently as part of the band's *Zoo TV Tour* stage set.

BILL WYMAN
CITROEN SM

An extraordinary car, this. How does a car with spats, and a chassis that appears way too big for its boots, work? But the SM does have its rock star fans. American musicians Cheech & Chong and Carlos Santana were owners when this very un-American-looking car first became available in 1970. And, not one but two Rolling Stones have purchased them. Although he doesn't drive, drummer Charlie Watts had one added to his collection and former bass player Bill Wyman (pictured) somehow looks a perfect fit for his SM.

KATE BUSH
FERRARI 308 GTS

This semi-convertible –Targa Top
– Ferrari was the backdrop for one
of the pictures taken during this
Italian Kate photoshoot in 1978.

ROD STEWART
ENZO FERRARI

Rod likes Ferraris. When interviewed
by *GQ* magazine he couldn't remember
exactly how many he owned.
"I've got Ferraris coming out me bum,"
he jested. "Must have four or five."
This little beauty is the Enzo Ferrari
named after Enzo Anselmo Ferrari, the
Italian racing driver, entrepreneur and
founder of the iconic car business.

HIGH ROLLERS

DIANA ROSS
ROLLS-ROYCE CORNICHE

An uncharacteristically casually turned out Diana perches on this immaculate North American Corniche.

MARVIN GAYE
ROLLS-ROYCE PHANTOM V

Marvin walks the streets of Notting Hill, London, back in 1976, followed by his Roller. *What's Going On*?

ELVIS PRESLEY
ROLLS-ROYCE PHANTOM

Elvis had more than one Roller. Posing with this one outside his Graceland home in Memphis, you get the feeling it might have been his favourite. It was certainly a tad less problematical than the blue model he had re-painted a lighter shade. Apparently, his mum's chickens would constantly peck at their reflections in the paintwork of the original Rolls.

IT'S A MAN'S WORLD

RUN-DMC
CADILLAC ELDORADO

Run-DMC look as though they pretty much own the neighbourhood as they perch atop this snowy white convertible. This is Hollis Avenue, New York City's hip-hop central. No parking problems for them. There's even a street nearby named Run-DMC JMJ Way in their honour.

JAMES BROWN
LINCOLN CONTINENTAL

"Put a Rolls-Royce grille on a Thunderbird" was the directive from on high by the Ford Motor Company to Design VP Eugene Bordinat. The result? This funky Lincoln Continental Mark III, which hit the production line in the late Sixties. This 1969 model, owned by James Brown, enabled The Godfather of Soul to arrive in style at the airport when boarding his Learjet.

PINK FLOYD: A NICE PAIR

SYD BARRETT
PONTIAC PARISIENNE

This huge American gas-guzzler might have made a handy prop for Mick Rock's photo session but its owner, Syd Barrett, hadn't a clue how to drive it. According to Rock, the Floyd legend's two-door convertible was the subject of a rock 'n' roll car swap. T.Rex bongo man Mickey Finn owned the car before Barrett and exchanged this rust bucket for Syd's Mini.

PINK FLOYD
GP BEACH BUGGY

Small cars were funky accessories in the Sixties. Not content with a Mini, Pink Floyd's Roger Waters, Syd Barrett, Nick Mason and Rick Wright found this functional buggy appealing. Although, judging by Roger, Syd and Rick's indifference, it was probably left to enthusiastic petrolhead Nick to suggest this photoshoot.

PINK FLOYD: NICK'S DELICATE SOUND OF THUNDER

NICK MASON
FERRARI 250 GTO

Said to have set the highest price at auction of any car, Nick's Ferrari (left) went for an eye-watering $34.65 million. It has history and a decent track record and is one of only 39 manufactured. In 1962, the year of its creation, Nick's former pride and joy raced at Le Mans, finishing third.

NICK MASON
AUTO UNION TYPE C

Nick got his love of motorsport from his amateur racing driver father Bill Mason, who wrote and directed the Shell Film Unit's acclaimed pre-war documentary *History of Motor Racing*. Bill's son is pictured (right) at the wheel of this 1936 German Auto Union, which he has raced at the Goodwood Festival of Speed.

SEDENTARY SEDANS

CAPTAIN BEEFHEART AND HIS MAGIC BAND
CADILLAC SERIES 62

The eccentric Captain, Don Van Vliet, was somewhat worryingly into fast cars. He owned a Hudson, Corvette and Jaguar but is pictured here on the bonnet of the Magic Band's capacious four-door Cadillac Series 62 sedan.

BOB DYLAN
CHEVROLET MASTER

Bob was more of a motorcycle man until his infamous 1966 accident aboard his Triumph 500 at Woodstock. Here he is pictured in a blaze of red leaves in the fall of 1968. This sedentary pose perched on the back of an unidentified vehicle was snapped by fellow Woodstock resident Elliott Landy. Best guess is that Bob or Elliott's rather London taxi cab-like mode of transport was a 1939 Master Deluxe Town Sedan.

PAUL WELLER
BMW MINI COOPER

A lover and driver of Minis throughout his life, Paul Weller jumped at the chance to design a one-off special model in 2010. A charity initiative benefitting Nordoff Robbins and War Child saw The Modfather create this candy-stripe car, echoing the look he created for a Ben Sherman shirt he designed a few years earlier.

BILLY GIBBONS
FORD THUNDERBIRD

Fresh out of the paint-and-body shop comes this old 1958 Ford Thunderbird owned by Billy Gibbons. The ZZ Top guitarist has a collection of more than 50 vehicles. Among them are a good number of hot rods, the mode of transport you might best associate with ZZ Top. But this beauty (right), dubbed 'Mexican Blackbird', he had transformed for driving at a more leisurely pace around California.

IT'S A MAN THING...

DAVID RUFFIN
MYSTERY BLACK SALOON

Okay - this is a book about cars, but who's concentrating on the make and model (far left)? Temptations soul singer David Ruffin stepped out of this black number straight into a pride of lions, and there's evidence to suggest that they were most definitely not stuffed!

BARRY GIBB
LOTUS EUROPA

Bee Gee-sus! The whole fabulous package: rock star owner, sporty, low-slung Lotus and engine fully exposed.

FREDDIE MERCURY
STUDEBAKER CHAMPION

He is the champion. Freddie gets first prize in the Rock Stars Cars' product placement competition as he makes himself comfortable on this 1950 Studebaker Champion.

CULT HEROES

DENNIS WILSON
CHEVROLET ONE-FIFTY

Dennis Wilson sits on the hood of the drag car that starred in the 1971 movie *Two-Lane Blacktop*. The Beach Boys' drummer was accompanied on this hot rod-battling road trip by fellow musician James Taylor and actors Warren Oates and Laurie Bird. 'No beginning, no end, no speed limit!' yelled the posters. The rather dull Chevrolet One-Fifty was the economy Chevy of its day and was only in production from 1953 to 1957.

GRAM PARSONS
CADILLAC ELDORADO

Gram Parsons opens up for the camera while posing on the hood of his Cadillac. The parking is spot on. The band he formed in 1968 were The Flying Burrito Brothers; his T-shirt says as much, and he's parked right outside the Burrito King restaurant on Alvarado and Sunset in Echo Park, LA.

PAINT JOBS

JANIS JOPLIN
PORSCHE 365

When Janis purchased this 1965 Porsche 365 Cabriolet second-hand in 1968, it was plain old white. She very quickly decided that the car needed jazzing up and persuaded her roadie, Dave Roberts, to give it a psychedelic finish. A year later it was stolen. What idiot would steal such a thing and not expect to draw attention? The same idiot who then proceeded to spray-paint it grey! But the most recognisable car in San Francisco was thankfully recovered and restored to its former glory. Now said to be worth $400,000 at auction, the car currently resides in the Rock and Roll Hall of Fame Museum in Cleveland.

THE KINKS
BUICK ELECTRA 225

This London photoshoot aboard their psychedelic Buick provided front-cover images for Kinks albums *Sunny Afternoon* and *Original Hits*.

SOME BODY TO LEAN ON

PAT BENATAR
NASH AMBASSADOR

Pat's 1955 Ambassador was one of those delightfully quirky cars that had a front end that looked half like a rear end.

BRIAN JONES
ROLLS-ROYCE SILVER CLOUD

Get off of my cloud: The Rolling Stones founder member purchased his vintage 1950s Roller from the 'opposition': Beatle George Harrison.

LIAM GALLAGHER
BRISTOL

With just one showroom (in Kensington, naturally), Bristol Cars have attracted business from Tina Turner, Bono and Liam Gallagher for their exclusive, hand-made vehicles. The company was originally a branch of major aircraft manufacturer the Bristol Aeroplane Company.

WHITE WALL STYLE

HANK WILLIAMS
CADILLAC

On show at The Hank Williams Museum in Montgomery, Alabama, Hank's 1952 Baby Blue Cadillac holds huge significance for his fans. America's most popular country singer died in the back seat on New Year's Day 1953 at a gas station stop in West Virginia while being driven to his next concert date in Ohio. Hank was just 29 when he died from what the original autopsy indicated was heart failure.

RY COODER
BUICK CONVERTIBLE

A 1939 yellow Buick was the star of Ry Cooder's LP cover for *Into the Purple Valley* in 1972. The inside gatefold shows Ry, wife Susan and the Buick (which was borrowed from the couple's neighbour) in trouble with a flat rear tyre. The iconic front cover was shot in a fake rainstorm on a Warner Brothers movie lot in Hollywood.

FERRARIS NEW & OLD

ERIC CLAPTON
FERRARI SP12 EC

This 2012 special one-off Ferrari was made for guitar god Eric Clapton by basing the design on the 458 Italia and adding styling inspired by the three 1970s 512 BB's he has owned. Not surprisingly, Eric was pretty chuffed with the finished result. "One of the most satisfying things I've ever done" was how he later described the project.

J. GEILS
FERRARI 250 GT SPYDER CALIFORNIA SWB

Guitarist and founder of the Massachusetts blues-rock outfit The J. Geils Band, John 'J' Geils has always loved Italian-made cars. This little beauty is just one of many cars he has collected in his bid to secure all five (Ferrari, Alfa, Lancia, Maserati and Fiat) of the great Italian marques.

FUN, FUN, FUN

BRIAN WILSON
CHEVROLET CORVETTE STINGRAY

You can't be too over-protective when you own a muscle car as beautiful as this little Corvette Stingray convertible. Repelling all invaders is Beach Boy Brian Wilson in the garage of his Beverly Hills property.

ROY ORBISON
EXCALIBUR ROADSTER

Roy Orbison looks quite the English country gent as he poses for a record cover in his Excalibur. The open-to-the-elements and doorless design didn't discourage other fans of the Milwaukee-manufactured car. Among those seen out and about in the exclusively limited number of Excaliburs that have come off the production line include Rod Stewart, Sonny Bono, Cher, Paul Revere, Bobby Darin and Liberace.

TAKIN' IT EASY

GLENN FREY
CHEVROLET BEL AIR

Eagles founder member Glenn Frey looks cool, but his beer might not be! This 1955 Chevy two-door hardtop, he affectionately called 'Gladys', is not to be confused with the car featured in the Eagles track 'Ol' '55', from 1974 album *On the Border*. The song was penned by Tom Waits and that's another car story for another day.

JACKSON BROWNE
CHEVROLET BEL AIR

Look right and here's 'Gladys' again. Glenn Frey generously made a present of Gladys to friend and fellow rock star Jackson Browne. Both had collaborated on the writing of the Eagles' big breakthrough hit 'Take it Easy' some while back, and then Browne had the car 'titled' with the name of his new album. In the end, this shot of Gladys never made it on to the final cover.

THE
COLLECTORS

JAY KAY
FIVE FAVOURITES

When *Daily Telegraph Motoring* quizzed Jay Kay on his favourite cars he came up with these five from his collection of more than 50. Clockwise from the centre, they are: Aston Martin DB6 Mark 1, BMW 2002 Bauer Cabriolet, Ferrari Vignale 330 GT, Mercedes-Benz 300SL Roadster and Porsche 911 2.7 RS, of which he says, "You won't get a better rock star colour than this!"

NEIL YOUNG
ON THE LOOK-OUT

Neil's Broken Arrow Ranch in California boasts a decent sized collection of classics. A 200-yard area includes a heap of rusting vehicles which he admits are "all totalled". An automobile graveyard is an apt description. Neil's favourite car? He's dubbed the '47 Buick Roadmaster sedan (Fastback) as "probably the most beautiful".

CAR CEMETERY

ALEX CHILTON
CADILLAC SERIES 62

The former lead singer in
The Box Tops and Big Star
leans against a car that
wouldn't look out of place in
Neil Young's car graveyard.

CREEDENCE CLEARWATER REVIVAL
SHELBY COBRA
FIAT 128

The car equivalent of Boot Hill
awaits these sorry specimens.
No, not Creedence, who clearly
found the perfect location for
a typical late-Sixties counter
-culture photo session, but the
deceased vehicles they are
using to promote themselves.
Surely that can't be an Austin
1100, can it? What kind of car
importer would bring in Britain's
favourite Seventies family run-
around to the US West Coast?

HIT THE ROAD, JACK

THE ROLLING STONES
CADILLAC ELDORADO BIARRITZ

Mick Jagger takes the wheel as the Stones drive towards the Brooklyn Bridge as part of an NYC promotion for their 1997 *Bridges to Babylon Tour*. Balanced on Keith Richards' knees is a ghetto blaster, which he would lift up blaring out the latest Stones tracks once Mick had parked the 1955 Caddy near a stage at the foot of the bridge.

ERIC CLAPTON AND BB KING
CADILLAC ELDORADO CONVERTIBLE

The best second-hand car advert ever! Eric driving BB was a photoshoot for the cover of their 2000 album together, *Riding with the King*. The idea was Eric's and, as it turns out, so was the black 1966 Cadillac, which was for sale.

PHOTO OPPORTUNITY

THE DOORS
RAMBLER CLASSIC 660 STATION WAGON

Stop boys! Out you get. A perfect spot for the latest photo of Jim Morrison and the band pays off. A few minutes after this picture was taken, the money shot was bagged and became the cover of The Doors' 1968 LP *Waiting for the Sun*. Then it was back in the Rambler and back down Laurel Canyon.

TOM JONES
ROLLS-ROYCE PHANTOM V

When you've got it, flaunt it! When Tom Jones made it big in the Sixties he returned to the street in Wales where he spent his youth with a big cigar and an even bigger Roller. It's hard to tell whether his former neighbour in the background is pleased for him or just concerned about his parking.

STING, BILL, ELVIS AND THE MGS

STING
MGB GT

It's that moment when you finally have enough cash to splash on a decent set of wheels and leave a succession of old bangers behind. Proud owner of this 1968 MGB GT, the Police man points at one of the most iconic badges in British motoring.

BILL WYMAN
MGB ROADSTER

Rolling Stone Bill smoulders on the bonnet of his MG and, like Sting, draws attention to that MG badge.

ELVIS PRESLEY
MG MGA ROADSTER

Elvis appears to lose control of his MGA while filming his 1961 movie *Blue Hawaii*. Impressed with the little car, he kept it for a few years until giving it to his secretary.

HAVE AXE, WILL TRAVEL

THE MARSHALL TUCKER BAND
PONTIAC FIREBIRD

This photo of the band was snapped for a rum advertisement. The white 1982 Pontiac Firebird was the grand prize in the competition which described the vehicle as "a stereo on wheels".

JOE WALSH
MASERATI

Joe's autobiographical hit song 'Life's Been Good' has the killer line: "My Maserati does 185." His number plate is presumably the closest he could get. Check out all the other Maseratis online with variations on this licence plate.

JOHN LEE HOOKER
BUICK SKYLARK

The licence plate on this 1953 Buick Skylark featured on the Mississippi bluesman's 1991 album cover and provided its title.

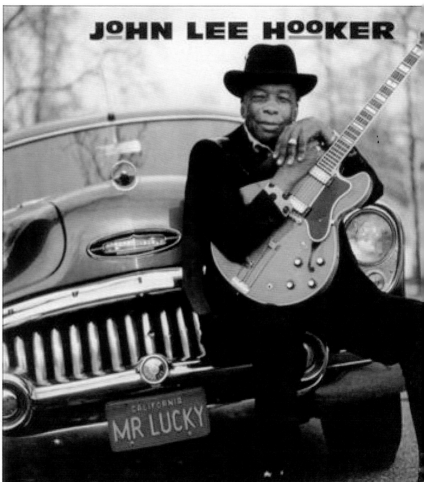

JOHN LEE HOOKER

SITTIN' ON MY CAR

BEYONCE AND JAY Z
CHEVROLET IMPALA CABRIOLET DELUXE

The happy couple ride around Cuba in this beautiful 1964 Chevrolet, which you too can hire for your sightseeing trip to Havana.

USHER
MERCEDES A45 AMG

Usher loves Mercedes – so much so that when the singer-songwriter and actor first made it big he bought his mum one. Recently he plumped for a 2014 Mercedes SLS AMG and travelled all the way to the Mercedes production plant in Germany as an invited guest to have some fun helping to assemble a V8 engine. Here, he's pictured on the Affalterbach track before road-testing the company's A45 AMG.

STRETCH MERCEDES

DAVID BOWIE
MERCEDES-BENZ 600 PULLMAN

The Thin White Duke might not have been much of a petrolhead but he knew a photo opportunity when he saw one. Nineteen gigs into his 1976 *Station to Station Tour*, Bowie arrives at Victoria Station, having departed the boat train to make his grand entrance for press and fans standing in the back of this Mercedes Pullman. "Heil and Farewell" mischievously reported the *New Musical Express* at the time - a thinly veiled headline suggesting that Bowie might have been making Nazi salutes.

PETE TOWNSHEND
MERCEDES-BENZ 600

Pete once claimed it took him five years to save up for this, his favourite Mercedes. And then the parking problems began...

BLUES BROTHERS

THE BLUES BROTHERS
DODGE MONACO SEDAN

The star of 1980 movie *The Blues Brothers* was this six-year-old 440 Dodge Monaco, cast as The Bluesmobile. The film-makers purchased the 13 Dodge cop cars required for the movie from the California Highway Patrol. That was but a quarter of the total number of police vehicles used in the movie, and so many were trashed during filming that a world record was set for most cars destroyed in one film, a record which stood until broken during the shooting of sequel *Blues Brothers 2000*!

LITTLE JUNIOR PARKER
CADILLAC DE VILLE

Smooth bluesman Little Junior Parker shows off a Caddy in a picture taken for the cover of his 1962 LP *Driving Wheel*. Let's hope he got to keep the car.

A PAIR OF CADILLACS

DEBBIE HARRY
FORD THUNDERBIRD

Flash car - flash Harry! The 1970s, when this model was in production, heralded a re-think in the size of American gas guzzlers, but Ford's Thunderbird still had it large.

DOLLY PARTON
CADILLAC DE VILLE

A smouldering Dolly Parton packs a few frocks and a trunk full of guitars ready for another tour. She's ridden in a few Cadillacs since this picture was snapped. Her 1997 Cadillac d'Elegance was a favourite and is now on display, complete with autographed arm rests, at the Hollywood Star Cars Museum.

COOL MILES

MILES DAVIS
FERRARI 275 GTB

Jazz trumpeter Miles Davis and his car stories could fill a book. He would famously race friends, such as Thelonius Monk, in the early hours of a New York City morning and even attempt to outrun the local cops, on one occasion with a terrified Jimi Hendrix in the passenger seat. The Ferrari (left) was quite possibly the one he was arrested in back in 1970 for possession of brass knuckles, or perhaps the one he was attacked in – shot in the hip a year earlier.

MILES DAVIS
LAMBORGHINI MIURA

This was the green Lamborghini Miles totalled during a risky driving manoeuvre in 1972, breaking both ankles in the process. Although hospitalised for a lengthy period and unable to perform, he couldn't bear to be without a Lamborghini and quickly purchased another.

LARGER THAN LIFE!

RINGO STARR
CHEVROLET BEL AIR

Ringo appears to be indicating that he's been the proud owner of at least two Chevy Bel Airs. And indeed he has. This one is the classic sedate version. The world's most famous drummer also took delivery of a flame-yellow and black customised model – a copy of one made in his honour and called the Chevrolet Bel Air Ringo Starr.

ALICE COOPER
CHEVROLET BEL AIR

Alice's gesture says it all. The front end of the Bel Air might have been relatively sober, but have you ever seen fins like these?

OZZY AND SHARON OSBOURNE
OLDSMOBILE FUTURAMIC

The Osbournes have their own kind of garage sale and auction off Sharon's 1950 Oldsmobile Futuramic 88 for charity.

OLD SCHOOL

ROD STEWART
ROLLS-ROYCE

Britain's most-photographed couple for some years in the Seventies, Rod Stewart and Britt Ekland pose by their latest mode of transport, a 1920s Rolls-Royce.

BRIAN JOHNSON
BENTLEY VANDEN PLAS LE MANS TOURER

The AC/DC singer really knows a thing or two about cars. He even fronts his own TV show on the subject. So, what's his favourite car? Perhaps surprisingly, it turns out to be this fabulous 1928 4.5-litre Bentley that Brian affectionately calls 'Thunder Guts'. The Vanden Plas Le Mans Tourer even gets to go on the road with AC/DC so Brian can enjoy a fast-driving experience between gigs. "It oozes Britishness," he says proudly, and admits, "I drive it like I've just stolen it!"

ON THE ROAD AGAIN

BRUCE SPRINGSTEEN
CHEVROLET CORVETTE

A passenger's-eye view of the inside workings of The Boss's Corvette. The 1960 convertible was Springsteen's first Corvette but not his last. He obviously has a thing about the powerful little car named after the description given to small warships. These days Bruce can be seen out and about in a Corvette Stingray.

TEARS FOR FEARS
FORD MUSTANG

Looking cool! When Tears for Fears needed transport for their 'Everybody Wants to Rule the World' video in 1985, Roland Orzabal and Curt Smith drove around California in an Austin-Healey 3000. For the proper West Coast driving experience here they are in a fetching pink 1966 Mustang convertible.

ELTON vs ROD

ELTON JOHN
FERRARI DINO 246

It's the early Seventies and Elton's career has just skyrocketed. So, what do you do? Why, have your photo taken while perched on the bonnet of a Dino 246, of course.

ELTON JOHN
JAGUAR E-TYPE

In the drive of his home in Old Windsor, Elton creates his very own traffic jam. The E-Type gets pole position, with its personalised number plate representing "OK Elton".

ROD STEWART
FERRARIS

There was always friendly rivalry between Elton and Rod, and no doubt their latest cars became the topic of much banter. Rod loves his Ferraris. Despite enjoying driving around London in one, he admits that when faced with a tight spot he sometimes gets wife Penny to park for him.

SHARKS AND STINGRAYS

SLASH
CHEVROLET CORVETTE STINGRAY

Have guitar, will travel: Guns N' Roses axeman Slash looks joined at the hip to his 1966 big-block Corvette Stingray. But sadly all good things must come to an end and, having collected too much stuff, he decided to sell his "monster of a car", as he described it. Now he tootles around LA in nothing more exciting than an Aston Martin!

SHARKS
PONTIAC LE MANS

To promote the band name, guitarist Chris Spedding (far right) customised his Pontiac by adding a roof fin and shark teeth to the front. Sharks (also featuring, left to right, Steve 'Snips' Parsons, Marty Simon and Andy Fraser) then drove the shark car up to Beachy Head for this 1973 photo opportunity.

CELEBRITY ENDORSEMENT

KYLIE MINOGUE
LEXUS CT 200H

"The world's first full hybrid luxury compact car" was how Kylie plugged this Lexus in TV commercials. The pop star received her own personally specified model of the hatchback and drove the car throughout 2011 before generously auctioning it (complete with autographed headrests) for charity.

BOB DYLAN
CADILLAC ESCALADE

Bob never does anything you expect him to do. So why the surprise and the fuss when he lent his still magnetic presence to this Cadillac commercial for their latest model in 2007? If Bob's selling out like some critics complain, he's certainly not loyal to only one manufacturer. More recently he completed yet another car ad, this time for Chrysler, which aired to 111.5 million TV Super Bowl viewers in 2014.

LIVING IN A BUBBLE

BRYAN FERRY
MESSERSCHMITT KR200

The famous German aircraft company was banned from producing its winged weapons of destruction after World War II and turned its attentions to producing these cute bubble cars. Despite the unbelievably cramped cockpit, Bryan Ferry still looks cool - or maybe just numb from the lack of leg room.

ELVIS PRESLEY
MESSERSCHMITT KR200

Elvis demonstrates just how tiny the Messerschmitt was. The King added the 200cc three-wheeler to his car collection in 1956 and drove the it for a year before gifting it to his local Memphis clothier, Bernard Lansky. The grateful tailor got it in exchange for all the clothes Elvis wanted in a two-hour sweep of his store.

BRITISH MARQUES

T.I.
BENTLEY MULSANNE

Hip-hop artist and actor T.I. salutes his Bentley Mulsanne. Said to be outrageously quick for a big car, this rappers delight, made in Crewe, will set you back around £230,000.

STEPHEN STILLS & PETER TORK
BENTLEY S

Stills and one-time Monkee Tork start an impromptu jam session on the roof of this classic British car outside the house they shared - party central by all accounts - in Studio City, LA.

BOB DYLAN
AUSTIN PRINCESS

When Bob Dylan toured the UK in 1966 he was regularly photographed and filmed with this very British mode of transport. The black Austin Princess was on loan from his buddies The Rolling Stones.

CATCH THEM IF YOU CAN

THE DAVE CLARK FIVE
JAGUAR E-TYPE

Five Go Mad in an E-Type: This one was used extensively as a getaway car for Dave and his girlfriend as they headed out of London and down to Devon in the 1965 Dave Clark Five movie *Catch Us If You Can*.

SAMMY HAGAR
FERRARI 599 GTB FIORANO

As you can see, Sammy Hagar gets a tiny bit excited whenever he's around Ferraris, and he's around them a lot. So obsessed is he with the sound of a 5000-rpm engine that he based his vocal scream and signature guitar tone on the blast and power of the Ferrari. After a tour he drives them. On vacation he goes hunting for them. The man should, surely, one day have a Ferrari named after him...

SHOPPING CARS

MUDDY WATERS
CADILLAC FLEETWOOD 60 SPECIAL SEDAN

That's Muddy Waters about to take the wheel of a 1955 Cadillac Fleetwood 60 Special Sedan. Muddy and the three other noted bluesmen (left to right: Otis Spann, Hubert Sumlin, Muddy and James 'Killer' Triplet) have just paid a visit to the Jones Hotel, Memphis.

ELVIS PRESLEY
CADILLAC ELDORADO SEVILLE

He's just popped into town to get his hair cut at Jim's Barber Shop on Main Street, Memphis, and a cop appears to write Elvis out a ticket for his new white Cadillac. It's unknown whether he's tucking a bribe into the officer's pocket or just crossing his fingers. Maybe it was all a stunt - but it made for an excellent photo moment and the opportunity to highlight one of Elvis's lesser-known cars.

FLORIDA RIDAS

TRIPLE C'S
ROLLS-ROYCE PHANTOM

Custom Cars & Cycles was the debut album by Florida hip-hop quartet Triple C's. The cover of the 2009 release had the boys all over a bunch of motorcycles, so here they are with some cars which definitely ain't custom.

FLO RIDA
BUGATTI VEYRON

Another Florida rapper with expensive taste. Flo Rida looks like he's telling the man with the camera where to go as he proudly guards his mirror chrome Bugatti. Not content with the chrome makeover, the car, which some say is the world's fastest, has now been goldified. Purchased at an eye-watering $1.7 million even before going gold, is it any wonder the man is protective?

UNION JACK BANDS

SCREAMING LORD SUTCH
ROLLS-ROYCE SILVER WRAITH

"I was driving down Sunset in my Union Jack car / I got stuck in the traffic, I didn't get far," screamed Lord Sutch on the track 'Union Jack Car'. That Sutch decided to decorate his elegant 1955 Roller with the British flag was a sign of things to come: he became a national institution as founder of the UK's Monster Raving Loony Party from 1983.

THE WHO
VOLVO P1800

Before Volvo gained a reputation for reliable but dull family cars, it produced some snappy Sixties gems. Driven by Roger Moore in TV's *The Saint*, the P1800 was also the choice of a 21-year-old Roger Daltrey, who splashed out on one with his £500 cash advance for The Who's second album, *A Quick One*.

CUSTOM CARS

JEFF BECK
FORD DEUCE COUPE

Jeff Beck shot to fame in The Yardbirds during the Sixties, released two hit solo albums in the Seventies, and then became a world-class, guitar-toting session man. But he also loves his cars, and he hot-rods (modifies and rebuilds) old vehicles – like this 1932 Ford. "My mum made a mistake of buying me a hot rod magazine to keep me quiet one day," he explained. "And, once that sets in as a six-year-old, you've had it!" In fact, he introduced Eric Clapton to classic hot rods.

GENE SIMMONS
BARRIS CUSTOM

The legendary custom-car maker George Barris gave us TV's original Batmobile, the 'Munster Koach' (from *The Munsters*) car and various KITTs (in *Knight Rider*). Gene Simmons, of KISS, is a big fan of Barris' work, and poses here with a *Munsters*-inspired creation.

OPEN-TOP TYPES

THE EVERLY BROTHERS
FERRARI 250 CALIFORNIA SPYDER

The close-harmony siblings Don and Phil Everly once recorded a song called 'Always Drive a Cadillac', in which they sing "I'll always drive a Cadillac and I'll always drink champagne." Well, maybe they did always drink champers, but they're breaking that Cadillac rule here: that would appear to be a Ferrari that they're driving.

JOHNNY CASH
CADILLAC ('49–'70)

This Frankenstein's monster of a Cadillac was built to promote Johnny Cash's song 'One Piece at a Time'. The song's about an assembly-line worker who steals a Cadillac by taking one piece at a time home in his lunchbox. Nashville mechanic Bruce Fitzpatrick (far right) constructed the car from Cadillac parts, using the song as a manual.

JIMI'S CARS

JIMI HENDRIX
LOTUS ELAN

To be precise, this is a Lotus Elan S3 Fixed Head Coupe, introduced in 1965. It's a sleek, zippy little beauty that is right at home in Swinging Sixties London. In fact it was the car driven by the character Emma Peel in the TV series *The Avengers*. This Lotus didn't actually belong to Jim Hendrix, but to Noel Redding, his bassist).

JIMI HENDRIX
DODGE PICK-UP TRUCK

You couldn't get more of a contrast:than between a Lotus Elan and a Dodge pick-up truck. A year after this photo was taken, Hendrix was party to a little truck thievery with Neil Young and his attorney on their way to the Woodstock Festival. Their plane landed at the wrong airport and, with no transport, Young's attorney stole a truck to get them to the gig. "Stealing a pick-up truck with Hendrix is one of the high points of my life," Young once admitted.

TO BE FRANK...

THE MOTHERS OF INVENTION
A FAMILY SALOON

'Do you like my new car?' asked Frank Zappa in his song of the same name, from 1970. It's hard to tell whether we like his new car or not in this pic, seeing as his band, self-proclaimed 'freaks' The Mothers of Invention, are hogging all the pavement for a spontaneous conga-chain and can-can dance.

FRANK ZAPPA
D-7 TRACTOR

We're Only in it for the Money was the title of one of Frank Zappa's albums. But if you're a rock 'n' roll satirist with an oddball sense of humour, no flashy sports car or limousine will cut it. For an interview with *Rolling Stone* in 1968, Zappa leapt aboard this old Caterpillar D-7 tractor, found rusting among old road-grading equipment in the hills of Laurel Canyon, above his house in Los Angeles.

MOTÖRHEAD
FORD CAPRI

Phil ('Philthy Animal') Taylor, Lemmy and 'Fast' Eddie Clarke proudly display their Ford Capri's custom paint job in 1981. The fanged-face band logo, with huge tusks and chains, is affectionately known as "War-Pig" or "Snaggletooth" to Motörhead fans. Let's hope nobody was driving at the time!

ISAAC HAYES
STUTZ BLACKHAWK

Superfly guy Isaac Hayes was Seventies soul music's smoothest, suavest, bad-assed brother. With lapels that big and flares that wide, you're going to need a motor that won't be overshadowed – and Hayes' Stutz Blackhawk did the job. Hayes wasn't alone in digging the Bearcat: it was also beloved of Sammy Davis Jr and Dean Martin. Clearly a top choice if you were smooth and on the move.

CAR COLLECTOR

NEIL YOUNG AND DANIEL LANOIS
LINCOLN CONTINENTAL

This 1959 Lincoln Continental is unique. It is in fact a 'LincVolt': it is powered by batteries and a biodiesel-powered generator. Young has painstakingly converted his vehicle into the world's sleekest hybrid car. A proud owner, he shows it off here with his record-producer friend Daniel Lanois. However, the LincVolt caught fire in 2010, due to a fault with the battery charger in his garage.

NEIL YOUNG
CHRYSLER MONARCH BUSINESS COUPE

This weatherbeaten old-timer has certainly clocked a fair few miles. And the car's pretty old too. Dating from 1948, it's three years younger than Neil himself. A classic that would be perfect if he ever decided to change career to 1940s-style private detective.

CAR PROPS

JOE STRUMMER
DESOTO FIREDOME SPORTSMAN

The Clash's lead singer was a diehard fan of the classic American rock 'n' roll look, from leather jackets to the Elvis-style lettering on the *London Calling* album. Here, Strummer poses next to a 1958 DeSoto Firedome Sportsman.

NOEL GALLAGHER
NISSAN FIGARO

Nissan are not exactly top of the list when it comes to glamour and rock 'n' roll. However, there's something quite Britpop about this car's look, recalling the Datsun Fairlady models of the Sixties.

MICK FLEETWOOD
1939 PACKARD

Everyone's favourite lanky drummer, Mick Fleetwood, perches on one of America's classiest ever luxury cars. If Dr Who ever presented a *Bugsy Malone*-themed *Top Gear*, it might look something like this...

SOME BODY TO LEAN ON

TOM PETTY
JAGUAR XJS

Who says romance is dead? Tom Petty, the silver-tongued charmer, asked his wife, back when they were first dating, what her favourite car was. He then ordered this champagne convertible Jaguar XJS and it was delivered to his house the next day.

LED ZEPPELIN
JAGUAR XK150

In December 1968, Led Zeppelin had just signed their first record deal and had been paid an unprecedentedly huge advance. They don't look too happy about it, despite being able to afford a gorgeous Jaguar XK150.

WILLIE NELSON
DODGE PICK-UP

The country legend (as Uncle Jesse in the movie *The Dukes of Hazzard*) proves that real men sport a ponytail, backed up by a big blue Seventies Dodge pick-up truck.

ROLLIN' NO MORE

STEVEN TYLER
1956 MERCEDES 220 CONVERTIBLE

Even when you're the singer of Aerosmith, one of the biggest American rock bands of all time, you still have days when the car won't start. Pictured here on the outskirts of Boston, the battery of Tyler's Merc has just died. Photographer Ron Pownall explains: "The Benz wouldn't start. Steve got all greased-up, looking through the Mercedes manual. A tow-truck was called. The driver was a funny guy who mixed it up with Steve, threatening to hook-up that 'piece of junk' and tow it back to the shop. Steven said, 'No you're not!' Ultimately, he got out the cables and jump-started it."

TAYLOR SWIFT
1949 DODGE WAYFARER

Taylor has sold more than 8.5 million copies of her album *1989*, So the Dodge Wayfarer she's using as a recliner is a whole four decades older than her.

4 x 4

TED NUGENT
FORD BRONCO

Ted Nugent's idea of a good time isn't to stay on the road, but to blast off cross-country as fast as possible going no place in particular. Here he is, a bumpy ride away from his farm in Jackson, Michigan, leaning on his 1966 Ford Bronco, as photographer Ron Pownall manages against all the odds to get this shot for *Rolling Stone* magazine; without his light meter - shattered on the ride across Ted's cornfield.

RONNIE LANE
LAND ROVER

Having opted for a rural lifestyle, he stopped getting in the band's Learjet during their 1973 US tour, and started driving to the gigs by Range Rover with his wife and baby. He then bought himself a farm in a small village on the border of Wales. It looks like having moved their he decided on extra horsepower.

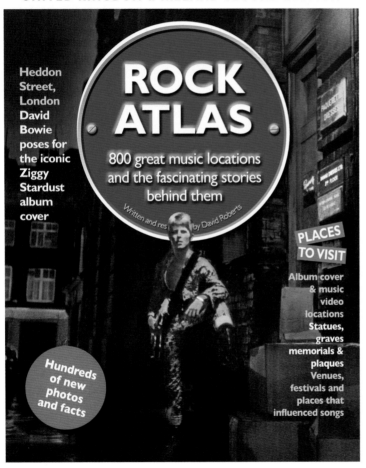

Heddon
Street,
London
David
Bowie
poses for
the iconic
Ziggy
Stardust
album
cover

ROCK ATLAS

800 great music locations
and the fascinating stories
behind them

Written and researched by David Roberts

PLACES TO VISIT

Album cover
& music
video
locations
Statues,
graves
memorials &
plaques
Venues,
festivals and
places that
influenced songs

Hundreds
of new
photos
and facts

Rock Atlas is more than just a guide to over 800 music locations. You can visit many of the places or simply enjoy reading this extraordinary fact-packed book's fascinating stories. Some are iconic, others are just plain weird or unusual, such as Bob Dylan turning up unannounced on a public tour of John Lennon's childhood home or the musical park bench commemorating Ian Dury's life that plays recordings of his hits and his appearance on Desert Island Discs.

Providing insights into many performers' lives, Rock Atlas includes artists as diverse as The Beatles, Sex Pistols, Lady Gaga and Lonnie Donegan. Presented in an easy-to-read, region-by-region format, every entry provides detailed instructions on how to find each location together with extensive lists of the pop and rock stars born in each county.

Illustrated with hundreds of rare, unseen and iconic colour and black and white photographs, Rock Atlas is a must for anyone with an emotional tie to contemporary music and the important places associated with it.

SE10
The record-breaking O2

Once famously dubbed a hugely expensive white elephant, London's Millennium Dome was regenerated by AEG Europe as the world's most popular music arena, overtaking New York's Madison Square Garden's record for most tickets sold in a year. Imagine turning the O2 structure upside-down as a giant dish: O2 boffins have calculated that it would take Niagara Falls 15 minutes to fill it with water or, if you prefer, 3.8 billion pints of beer. In addition to the 20,000-capacity arena, the O2 boasts nightclubs, cinema screens and a curving mall of eateries. Sadly, the once excellent interactive museum of popular music called the British Music Experience, which opened in 2009 closed in 2014. The whereabouts of the collection of handwritten lyrics, memorabilia and famous outfits from 60 years of British music history may pop up elsewhere, but at the time of writing plans were sketchy.

LOCATION 176: with access by tube, road and river, the O2 lies in a bend in the Thames at Peninsula Square, Greenwich, postcode SE10 0DX

The magnificent O2 attracts all the biggest international touring performers. Nine Inch Nails, the Eagles and Lady Gaga were just three of the acts which played the arena in 2014

Colorado

Morrison
Red Rocks Amphitheater

The possibilities presented by the rock formations in this part of Colorado for a dramatic natural outdoor amphitheater were realised by Jefferson County businessman John Brisben Walker in 1906. Beginning with a brass band concert, Brisben Walker's vision has changed little now that Red Rocks attracts some of rock's biggest names to the venue's capacity of 9,450. They don't come much bigger than The Beatles, who played Red Rocks on August 26 1964. Still relatively unfamiliar with outdoor performances, John, Paul, George, Ringo, manager Brian Epstein, and producer George Martin were, in the wake of almost constant death threats to the band, seriously concerned about the ease with which a sniper might take a shot at the stage from high up in the rocks. The Beatles were also unaccustomed to the high altitude at Red Rocks, and for moments when short of breath oxygen canisters were placed side of stage for their use. Despite breaking the then outdoor concert record attendance with a crowd of 7,000, unusually for The Beatles 2,000 of the tickets for this appearance remained unsold. The amphitheater has seen its fair share of controversy, particularly around the late sixties and early seventies when Aretha Franklin's no-show due to a contract dispute sparked rioting and the destruction of a piano. Then there was the tear-gassing of rioting crowds at the Denver Pop Festival in 1969 and the same police action at a Jethro Tull gig in 1971. Many Red Rocks concerts have made it on to record and film. U2 did both in 1983 when their Live at Red Rocks: Under a Blood Red Sky was released as a movie and two tracks from the band's

Right: where the Great Plains meet the Rocky Mountains - rock at Red Rocks Below: one of many to benefit from the Red Rocks experience were the Dave Matthews Band, whose Live at Red Rocks 8.15.95 album was certified double-platinum after peaking at #3 on the Billboard 200

memorable performance during the War Tour found their way onto the live album, Under a Blood Red Sky. And the photogenic venue continues to attract bands who want to be filmed in the breath-taking geological landscape. Mumford & Sons, like U2 before them, had reached a similarly high point with their popularity when their The Road to Red Rocks live concert DVD was released in 2012. Previous to that, in 2010, Widespread Panic overtook the Grateful Dead as the band with the most performances at Red Rocks. In June of that year they achieved their 35th sold-out concert.

Location 182: Morrison is about 15 miles west of the center of Denver. The Red Rocks Park & Amphitheater Visitor Center is at 18300 West Alameda Parkway, Morrison, CO 80465

Rock Atlas USA

THE MUSICAL LANDSCAPE OF AMERICA

ROCK ATLAS is more than just a guide to 650 music locations across the USA. You can visit many of the places by following the book's detailed instructions or simply just enjoy reading the fascinating, fact-packed stories behind each entry. Seek out the quirky record stores, find the iconic recording studios, make a pilgrimage to memorials and statues, check out the best festivals, and visit the exact spot where your favorite album cover was photographed. Rock Atlas USA will be your guide.

Providing a unique insight into musicians' lives and songs through the places linked to them, Rock Atlas USA includes stories featuring artists as diverse as The Beatles, Lady Gaga, Muddy Waters, Bruce Springsteen, Kings of Leon, and Otis Redding.

Illustrated with hundreds of rare, unseen, and iconic color and black and white photographs, Rock Atlas USA is a must for anyone with an emotional tie to contemporary music and the important places associated with it.

650 GREAT MUSIC LOCATIONS

ROCK ATLAS USA

David Roberts

The musical landscape of America

Album cover & music video locations

Venues, festivals, studios, & homes

Statues, graves, museums, memorials, & plaques

Exclusive interviews and more than 500 fascinating photographs

Crosby, Stills & Nash Cover shoot by Henry Diltz, West Hollywood, 1969

PLUS! THE BRILL BUILDING • DEAD MAN'S CURVE • THE JOSHUA TREE • PAISLEY PARK • AND MORE

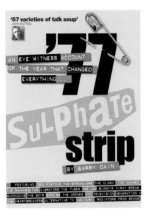
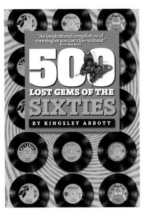
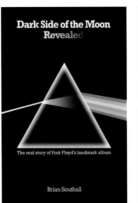
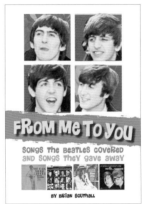
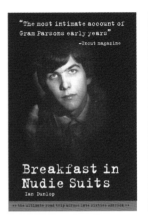

ES

The true story of Jimi's 15-month rise to fame
brand new insights from the people who knew him best

**Jimi Hendrix
Made in England**

by Brian Southall

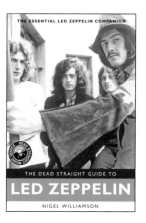

THE ESSENTIAL LED ZEPPELIN COMPANION

THE DEAD STRAIGHT GUIDE TO

LED ZEPPELIN

NIGEL WILLIAMSON

HIS LIFE & MUSIC IN ONE ESSENTIAL BOOK

THE DEAD STRAIGHT GUIDE TO

BOB DYLAN

NIGEL WILLIAMSON

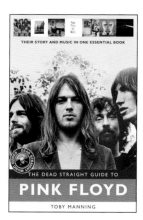

THEIR STORY AND MUSIC IN ONE ESSENTIAL BOOK

THE DEAD STRAIGHT GUIDE TO

PINK FLOYD

TOBY MANNING

ALL YOU NEED IS THIS! FROM FAB FOUR TO SOLO ARTISTS

THE DEAD STRAIGHT GUIDE TO

THE BEATLES

CHRIS INGHAM

for more great music books